Powder Puff Principles

Powder Puff Principles

A posh girl's guide to etiquette

National Indie Award Winning Author
KYM JACKSON

authorHOUSE®

AuthorHouse™
1663 Liberty Drive
Bloomington, IN 47403
www.authorhouse.com
Phone: 1-800-839-8640

Edited by Anne Dejoie-Lucas
and Peggy Bowen-Shawaker

PowderPuffPrinciples.com

Published by AuthorHouse   10/18/2012

ISBN: 978-1-4772-6836-0 (sc)
ISBN: 978-1-4772-6835-3 (hc)
ISBN: 978-1-4772-6837-7 (e)

Library of Congress Control Number: 2012916769

Contents

This book is dedicated to my sweet, loving mother,
Elouise, who encourages, supports,
and loves me unconditionally.

Powder Puff Principles: A posh girl's guide to etiquette
The second in a series of Powder Puff Principles® books by
Kym Jackson
Contributing Authors:
Elouise Jackson and Chauncey Jackson Walker

Posh \päsh\ : elegant or stylishly luxurious > *a*n upper-class way, talking posh quality or state of being elegant, stylish. **posh-ly — posh-ness**

Wiktionary.org

The second in a series of Powder Puff PrinciplesTM books

Powder Puff Principles

A posh girl's guide to etiquette

Good manners have always been based on common sense and thoughtfulness. This hasn't changed and never will. Think of etiquette not as a strict set of rules, but as a guideline for our natural instinct to incorporate kindness and consideration into everything we do.

—*Emily Post*

Crystle Stewart

Miss USA,

Actress, Model

Foreword

Despite our ever-changing world, some things remain constant. Manners, politeness, and an overall awareness of etiquette will never go out of style or be dismissed as "old-school." A smile, a thank you, or a proper tip for appreciated service still goes a long way and means a great deal. Putting our best foot—and face—forward is still a must each and every day of our lives, regardless of our age.

There is a proverb that says, "Train up a child in the way he should go: and when he is old, he will not depart from it." I believe we have to start teaching our children at an early age to respect themselves, take care of themselves, and be kind to others, no matter what. We have to not only tell them but also show them through our own words and actions how to be the best they can be. *Powder Puff Principles* provides an excellent vehicle for training in language that is easy to read and easy to understand. The book reminds one of the simple things in life that mean so much and can take us so far. I hope that as you read this book, you will be inspired to go out into the world and put into practice the techniques found here, so that you can put your best self forward in everything you do. Enjoy!

The only person who can talk you out of your greatness is you!

—AJ Johnson

*The difference between having a dream and living a
dream is what you do to make the dream reality.*

—AJ Johnson

Wearing the Crown

For me, wearing a crown really was a dream come true. Even as a child I was fascinated with the whole idea of beauty queens and pageants, and I dreamed of becoming Miss Texas and then Miss USA. I worked hard toward that goal, and I won first runner-up in the Miss Texas USA pageant, only to realize that time was running out for me to achieve my goal of wearing the Miss Texas crown. At age twenty-four, I became too old to continue competing in the "Miss" pageants. Apparently, twenty-four was over the hill! I realized that winning the crown in that particular pageant was just not going to happen in my life; I had to deal with that harsh reality and find comfort in knowing that I had done the best I could. But winning a pageant was still one of my heart's true desires.

While I had heard of the Mrs. Texas Pageant, I wasn't married at the time, so I couldn't compete. Fifteen years later and now married, I once again contemplated the idea of entering the pageant, but the timing was not right; though blissfully fulfilled by my new role as wife and mother to two very busy boys, my original dream was never far from my thoughts. Then one day, I just picked up the phone and called the Mrs. Texas USA Pageant—and the rest is history. My experience as Mrs. Texas 2005 was everything I dreamed of, and more! A quote by Pastor Joel Osteen sums it up: "You will produce what you're continually seeing in your mind." I saw myself as Mrs. Texas, something I really wanted! Ultimately, winning the crown became one of my greatest life accomplishments, not just because I won, but because I never gave up on a dream. And the journey involved in winning Mrs. Texas has been nothing short of incredible.

Never give up on your dreams and passions. Remember, you are just being groomed and fine-tuned to face the beautiful challenges of your future. Dream on . . .

Happiness is like perfume.
You can't give it away without getting a
little on yourself.

—Freya Stark

Hey, Girlfriends!

"Beauty is in the eye of the beholder." We've all heard this old cliché. The question is, What is the eye beholding—just physical attributes, or the many nuances that make up our total radiance?

I've been in the beauty business for more than twenty years, and my mother, Elouise, for thirty-plus years. Chauncey, my daughter, has given us insight into the questions and concerns of the younger generation. Over the past two decades, we have done seminars, workshops, and even a television program in which we openly addressed the issues and concerns surrounding beauty and etiquette.

Yes, beauty and etiquette are synonymous. You can have perfect features—a lovely smile, great eyes, beautiful skin—but if your social graces are inadequate, your total radiance still needs work. Many people are unaware of it, but true beauty is usually just an outward manifestation of inner beauty.

Over time, every successful woman accumulates wisdom comprised of Mom's teaching, Grandma's reminders, friends' discoveries, and an abundance of information gleaned from the pages of countless magazines, books, videos, and websites. *Powder Puff Principles* is no exception. It reflects our accumulated wisdom, much of which may have originated from sources now forgotten or misplaced. In that respect, the advice you read on these pages includes the time-honored wisdom of such luminaries as Tyra Banks, Donatello Versace, and Coco Chanel.

This book is a collection of observations, ideas, and suggestions compiled over many years. It is a generational collaboration—and I am very grateful to have a mother and daughter who make such wonderful collaborators!

Our simple wish is that the next time you ask, How should I . . . , When should I . . . , or Where should I . . . , you will find the answer in these pages. These basic educational principles never change, and they apply whether you're involved in a pageant, cotillion, or modeling—or just dressing for success.

So much of what we talk about in this book pertains to everyday lifestyle, etiquette, beauty, and simply treating others as you want to be treated. Our goal is to help make your day-to-day life just a little bit better. The advice here is like riding a bike: once you learn it, you won't forget it. You may get rusty over time, but with just a brief refresher, the knowledge returns quickly. Through practicing what you learn here, you will build your confidence in social situations and begin to define and improve your image for everyday living.

It is impressive to know your social graces. As a teenager, you may have thought that it was an old-fashioned notion for a woman to cook, set a table, and be beautiful and smart all at the same time. We hope that by now you have discovered that it is awesome to be a woman. We should embrace and nourish our femininity. Why shouldn't we be the best women we can be?

Don't let anyone rain on your parade

Sometimes we have to be stronger than we want to be, and we need to pull this strength from the core of our being. Challenging as they are, these are the times when we realize that all things are possible and that we deserve the best. The same is true when developing your sense of self, but in this case, you grow from the inside out. A strong inner core combined with a healthy mind and body can make you feel invincible.

You deserve to live a happy, healthy life, no matter your circumstances. As women, we have the ability to make lemonade from lemons. But, with a little inner strength, we can serve that lemonade in crystal goblets on a silver platter, with a smile from the soul. It's as easy as taking a stand and saying, "I should be different, and I am the person who is going to make the change."

Girlfriends, don't let anyone stop you from being the best person you can be. Sometimes the "rain" can bring out the very best in us, making us stronger than we ever imagined—and much, much more than we ever thought we could be!

It's good to be me!

A lot of women look in the mirror and find fault in what they see. Many of us spend precious time focusing on our every flaw. This is not healthy, and it could be dangerous to your self-esteem. Self-acceptance is looking in the mirror and saying, "I may have flaws, but I am still beautiful." Self-acceptance means loving the fact that you're unique and using what you have to be the most beautiful

7

woman you can be. It means disowning your flaws and embracing your assets.

Start by being your own cheerleader. Tell yourself, *Go, girl!* when you succeed and *That's okay* when you fail, realizing that at least you tried. It's saying, "Yes!" out loud—affirmation that you look and feel good, whether it's first thing in the morning when your hair is all messed up or after you've spent three hours getting dressed for a date. It's loving everything about you.

How do you do this? It's as easy as looking at yourself every time you get the chance and saying, "I love who you are—inside and out."

As the Bing Crosby songs goes, "You've got to accentuate the positive, eliminate the negative, and latch on to the affirmative. Don't mess with Mr. In-Between."

Becoming true to you

People stretch the truth daily when it comes to their age, weight, money, and more. But why do we lie to the one person who knows the truth—ourselves? Shakespeare said it best: "to thine own self be true." However, I'd like to add, "and then you can be true to others." Being honest starts from within, and it eventually evolves into wanting to be totally honest all the time.

Telling the truth is such a liberating experience that when you do it, even the skeletons in your closet will no longer haunt you. It isn't always easy to tell the truth; if it were, more people would do it. But honesty has its own rewards. Being an authentic woman is attractive and compelling. If dishonesty has become a bad habit and you want to become an honest person, start by admitting to yourself one truth a day. Then try two a day, until eventually you are being completely truthful all day, every day. Once you are honest with yourself, you will find it so much easier to be honest with others.

Be confident, even on those days when you don't feel it; no one has to know but you. Take deep breaths, smile, walk with assurance, and think before you speak. Body language says a lot, so stand tall and look people in the eye when you speak to them.

Be good to yourself first so you can be good to others. Learn to release anger or frustration in a constructive manner so you don't take it out on those around you. Most important, be willing and able to forgive yourself and others. Nobody's perfect.

Posh Tip: *When someone asks you a question you don't want to answer, smile and ask, "Why do you want to know?"*

I am a huge fan of personal hygiene,
so I embrace water!

—Jennifer Connelly

Hygiene Etiquette

Hygiene is simply being as fresh and clean as you can be. It is a very sensitive and personal subject for most people, but also very important. This is where your outer beauty gets to show off your light from within.

Hygiene is the first and most important part of not only your beauty regimen but also of caring for and loving your body. Look at it this way—these are things you already know; we're just giving a few little reminders that will keep you fresh and clean as whistle. No matter what you wear or how you fix your hair, your look will not come together if what is underneath is unpleasant. So here are some simple suggestions that will ensure your daily grooming is picture-perfect.

Teeth

One of the first things a person notices about you is your smile—your pearly whites. But you don't want your breath to be noticeable as well. An easy way to avoid this problem, especially if it results from a lengthy time lapse since your last brushing, is to chew a piece of sugarless gum; however, you should chew it for only a short period of time. Be careful not to swallow it, and by all means discard it properly by inconspicuously spitting it into a tissue or folding it back into the wrapper it came out of. Mints are your best option—keep them handy at all times. Mints come in such cute packaging these days; they could almost be considered an accessory! Gum may be an option sometimes, but typically it is not suitable for church, school, speaking or dinner engagements, or other more formal situations.

Mouth Grooming 101

These rules are essential to keeping teeth and gums healthy:

1. Brush your teeth at least twice a day, when you wake up and before you go to bed—especially if you have a sweet tooth!
2. Floss daily to remove plaque and the food between your teeth that brushing alone misses.
3. Use a mouthwash that is not too sweet, since sweet mouthwashes contain sugars that actually cause tooth decay.
4. See your dentist twice a year for cleanings.
5. Professional teeth whitening or over-the-counter whitening products are always options to explore. But be careful, because too-frequent whitening can destroy the enamel on your teeth.

6. Veneers, braces, and envisaging all are options for teeth that need to be straightened. With today's dental technology, your smile can be as beautiful as you want to make it.

Face and body

1. Cleanse your face daily, and don't forget your ears and neck.
2. Shower or bathe at least once a day. Think of ways to make bathing fun: a new bath oil or bubble bath, candles, music, etc.
3. Shave, wax, thread, or cream, to your level of tolerance, everywhere you have unwanted hair. If you're a young teen, talk to your mom, sisters, and friends to determine what is age-appropriate and acceptable. You don't have to take it all off, but by all means, keep it neat and under control.
4. A bikini wax is used to remove the hair from around your panty line. Have this done professionally; do not attempt to shave around this area, as it can be very uncomfortable and cause bumps and rashes.

Deodorant and antiperspirant

1. A deodorant deters only odor, not perspiration. An antiperspirant stops you from perspiring but not from having body odor. Make sure you get an antiperspirant deodorant that does both.
2. When wearing sleeveless tops, make sure the deodorant you use is colorless. It doesn't have to be seen for people to know you're wearing it.

3. Bodies sometimes become acclimated to a certain brand of deodorant, so find two or three that work for you and change products occasionally.
4. A feminine hygiene deodorant is as important as underarm protection. Use both.

Perfumes

Don't swim in your perfume. Be considerate of others.

Apply perfume only to pressure points: the wrists, behind the ears, inside the elbows, and behind the knees.

When using spray cologne, two or three squirts is plenty, and layering helps. Use the same fragrance in a bubble bath, moisturizing lotion, and spray cologne.

For best results, don't spray perfume directly onto your skin; spray it into the air and walk through it.

Menstrual hygiene

No woman feels totally comfortable during her period, but we must all endure it eventually, and so we should welcome it rather than feeling embarrassed. Menstruation is simply part of being a woman, so learn to accept it rather than run from it.

That said, your period can present a variety of challenges —premenstrual tension, bloating, cramps, and the logistics of dealing with a heavy flow. It is important to learn which forms of protection work best for you—sanitary pads, tampons, or menstrual cups. Whichever method you choose, make sure to change it regularly to avoid leaks, an unpleasant odor, and other problems.

You should know that tampons, especially, must be changed on a regular basis. If left inserted for excessive amounts of time, you increase the possibility of toxic shock syndrome (TSS). While all the causes of TSS have not been definitively proven, tampon usage has been linked to this deadly condition.

To help maintain a clean, fresh feeling, frequent washing is also important during "lady's time." Exterior washes and sprays may be used for added freshness, but we do not recommend the use of tampons or pads that contain deodorants, as these can cause irritation and other problems in some women that might require medical attention.

Q & A

Q: Is it possible to "over-bathe?"
A: Yes, and it falls under the category of "too much of a good thing." The biggest danger of over-bathing is dehydrating your skin and removing its natural oils, which will cause it to become rough and scaly.

Q: Why do my feet seem to have an odor so quickly after I shower?
A: After bathing, make sure to thoroughly dry your feet, especially between your toes, to avoid problems that cause foot odor.

Public hygiene

Public hygiene is also very important because it is seen by all who surround you. That includes not just how you present yourself but also how you act when out in public. It only takes one negative action to undo all of the beauty you display on the outside. Show consideration when you're out and about. Coughing out loud in public without covering your mouth and not washing your hands after a visit to the ladies' room are just a couple of many habits that portray you in a negative light. If you're walking your dog, always bring along a scoop and a catch-bag; never leave Fido's mess for others to step in or smell while on walks of their own. Spitting, cursing, loud burping, or flatulence are all no-no's and should be avoided in public at all cost. A good rule of thumb: if you wouldn't do it at home with your parents, don't do it in public. And treat those around you with the same respect you'd want to be shown.

Posh Tip: *Your body is a temple and should be treated as one. A few extra moments at the start of the day to make sure your hygiene is right can save a lot of embarrassment and explaining later on. A clean body evokes confidence!*

Every time you smile at someone, it is an action of love,
a gift to that person, a beautiful thing.

—*Mother Teresa*

Skin Care

I started my skin care regimen when I was nine years old. I remember my grandmother telling me that if you start taking care of your skin early, you will never have anything to worry about—no pimples, no wrinkles, no blemishes. Guess what? She was right! Grandmother knew something about the fountain of youth; she always took her vitamins and maintained a daily skin care program her entire life. When she was eighty-five, people didn't believe her when she would tell them her age. And apparently, her skin care lessons truly work because most people now have a difficult time guessing my age, or my mother's.

If you weren't lucky enough to have someone teach you good skin care techniques at an early age, it's never too late to learn.

Grandma's skin care regimen

1. Make a special effort to wash off your makeup in the evening, no matter how tired you are. Your skin needs to breathe at night.
2. Drink a lot of water. About 60 percent of our body is made up of—you guessed it—water. That means if it doesn't stay hydrated, it will dry and wrinkle like an un-watered houseplant.
3. Give yourself a simple facial once or twice a week. This fifteen minute focus can clean and rehydrate your skin, leaving it soft, smooth, and supple.
4. Begin by cleaning your face with a mild, high-quality facial soap. Next, soak a clean washcloth with warm (not too hot) water, and perhaps a touch of witch hazel or other astringent cleanser. Wring out the cloth, unfold it, and lay it over your entire face, allowing it to stay in place for a minute or two, and then gently rub off the cleanser using circular motions.
5. Follow this step with a good facial masque, or you can make your own from whipped avocado or oatmeal. A masque draws some of the harmful toxins from beneath the surface of the skin, deep-cleaning the areas where oil typically builds up.
6. Conclude with a good, non-greasy skin cream infused with alpha hydroxyl, made especially for use as a facial moisturizer. (Make sure to read the label carefully.)

What is your skin type?

1. Dry – flaking and peeling, feels tight after cleansing, and may also have a powdery, dull appearance. Drink lots of water; avoid excessive caffeine and alcohol. Use high-quality moisturizers frequently.

2. Oily – large pores, excessively shiny, frequent breakouts (pimples, blackheads, and/or whiteheads). Requires extra attention during cleansing. Mild astringents can help; avoid greasy moisturizers and makeup.
3. Sensitive – delicate, thin-looking, and prone to rashes, broken capillaries, and allergic reactions. Seek the counsel of a good dermatologist; ask for medications that are especially formulated for you.
4. Combination/Normal – This is what most people have: a combination of the other three types. Drink water, avoid excessive sun, and follow a daily cleansing regimen, including a weekly facial.

T-Zone

The T-zone is comprised of your forehead, nose, and chin. This area may be oily even though your cheeks and neck seem dry, making it prone to acne breakouts. Depending on your skin type, you may need to treat it differently than the rest of your face. For example, if you have dry skin don't use strong cleansers and toners, which will dry your skin ever more. If you have oily skin, use a cleanser that will deep-clean your face and an astringent that will alleviate some of the oil.

A word about astringents: some people think that the cure for oily skin is hot water and harsh alcohol astringents. But this often has the opposite effect, making your skin oilier as it compensates for the loss of moisture. Don't over-tone your face!

How to cleanse your face

Cleansing your face should be a multi-part process. Dampen your skin with lukewarm water, and then put some cleanser in the palm of your hand, remembering that a little goes a long way. Rub your hands together to create a small lather, and rub it gently into your checks, nose, forehead, neck, and chest to remove dirt and oil. Rinse with cool water to close the pores.

Next, tone your skin, using the gentlest toner you can find (alcohol-free). Apply over your entire face, avoiding the area around your eyes; cotton balls or cotton pads are ideal for this purpose.

Finally, moisturize. Use the best moisturizer that you can afford, and don't be afraid to try several until you find the one that is right for you. Apply sparingly over your entire face, including under your eyes. Don't forget your neck and chest, as they are also very important areas to maintain. If you practice this regimen faithfully, you will see its benefits well beyond your forties and fifties.

Homemade Mask for Dry Skin

- 1 avocado, peeled and seeded
- 2 teaspoons extra-virgin olive oil
- 2 cucumber slices

Mash the avocado and add olive oil. Apply to face. Place the 2 cucumber slices over the eyes. Leave on for 10 minutes, and then rinse with warm water. The cucumbers are an extra bonus to relieve dry, puffy eyes.

Mask for Oily Skin

- ¼ cup fine-ground oatmeal
- ½ cup water

- 1 teaspoon honey

Using a small but deep microwave-safe container, microwave the oats and water for 2 to 3 minutes on medium setting, until the mixture forms a thick paste. Allow mixture to cool to body temperature, and then stir in honey. Apply to face and leave for 15 minutes. Rinse off with lukewarm water.

For combination skin, which most of us have, either mask will work.

The most important skin care product is free

It is water, water, and more water! Drink a minimum of eight full glasses daily. I can't stress this enough. Water acts as a hydrating and cleansing agent. It washes out toxins and waste and will leave you feeling more enthusiastic and renewed. Water does not have to be ice-cold—in fact, many people find it easier to drink it at room temperature or even warm (which can be delicious with a twist of lemon). Keep a bottle in your car, locker or purse and sip it while you wait in traffic or between classes on the run.

To keep your skin looking radiant . . .

1. Reduce or eliminate caffeine. Coffee, tea, and chocolate are like diuretics and will dry your skin. Water is always your best choice of beverage, followed by natural juices and caffeine-free options.
2. Don't smoke. Not only is smoking a health risk, but the smoke, tar, and nicotine from cigarettes also cause dryness, especially around the facial area. If you doubt that, look

carefully at the skin of a lifelong smoker. Cigarettes also cause heart problems, lung cancer, and pregnancy complications, along with damage to skin and teeth. So add to your fresh, healthy, youthful look, and don't smoke!

Protect yourself from the sun. Are you aware that one out of every seven Americans will develop some form of skin cancer? Sun worshipers, beware! As the ozone layer protecting our atmosphere is depleting, cancer-causing ultraviolet light are able to penetrate it. You cannot be too aggressive in protecting yourself, and you should always apply sunscreen before leaving home these days. Many makeup lines have added sunscreen into their products. Make it part of your daily regimen, just like your foundation, moisturizers, and lotions. Fresh air and sunshine are needed in moderation to replenish your vitamin D, but also consider a glass of fresh-squeezed orange juice for that extra boost.

Some skin care no-no's:

o   No body soap, detergent, or deodorant soap on your face.
o   No rubbing alcohol on your face unless advised by a medical professional.
o   No really hot water on your face, unless you are having a steam facial.

Q & A

Q: If it is a cloudy day, do I still need to wear sunscreen?
A: Yes. The sun rays penetrate right through clouds and fog, as well as automobile glass. It can even penetrate deep water.

Q: I am African-American. Do I still need to use sunscreen?
A: Yes. Some of the strongest and most harmful rays still penetrate even the thickest of clouds. Just because you are a person of darker color does not mean you do not need protection. Your skin is just as sensitive and susceptible to disease as that of anyone else.

Posh Tip: *Remember the three Rs: Respect for self, Respect for others, and Responsibility for all your actions.*

To eat is a necessity, but to eat intelligently is an art.

—François de la Rochefoucauld

Beauty for Life

Skin care is a great way to put your best face forward—from the outside. But creams and cleansers don't do much for the inside! The first secret to a beautiful you is a fit, healthy lifestyle. And diet and exercise are the keys to a healthy and beautiful body, mind, and soul. Start while you're young to make good nutrition and fitness a way of life. Learn to make heart-healthy food choices at an early age, and combine a good diet with a regular exercise program that you can rely on for a lifetime.

Most of us have been taught to "clean our plates." But the fact is, it's okay if you don't always eat everything you're served. When you feel full, stop eating.

How often you eat is just as important as how much you eat. Having one large meal a day is not healthy. It can cause fatigue and blood-sugar imbalances, not to mention the fact that your body's metabolism will slow down because it's trying to conserve energy until the next meal. Three nutritious meals with two to three smart snacks will keep your body and mind well-fueled, alert, and properly metabolized throughout the day.

Breakfast has always been considered the most important meal of the day. You "break the fast" your body has been undergoing overnight as you sleep. Here are some healthy food suggestions, beginning with that most important meal.

Breakfast

Fresh fruit
grapefruit
strawberries
bananas
apples
melons

Whole wheats
oatmeal
cream of wheat
malted meal
granola bars
grain/corn cereals
whole-wheat breads
muffins with light butter, honey, agave, peanut butter, or
small amount of jam

Proteins
turkey
chicken
hard-boiled or scrambled eggs

Dairy
low-fat yogurt
protein shakes

Beverages
fresh-squeezed juices
tomato juice or any vegetable juice
green tea, hot or cold
decaf coffee
skim milk
Crystal Light

Posh Tip: When it comes to fruits and vegetables, fresh is best, frozen is next, and canned always comes last!

Lunch

Soups with clear broths and low sodium
Salads:
    fruit, grilled/broiled meats on mixed greens
    (the deeper color the greens, the more nutritional value)
Sandwiches:
    tuna, turkey, chicken, low-fat cheese, veggies, lettuce, tomatoes, fresh spinach, and cucumber

Supper

Meat:
    baked/broiled/grilled chicken, fish, beef, turkey (avoid fried foods)

Vegetables:
broccoli
spinach
squash
cabbage
green beans
carrots
cauliflower

Starches:
baked potatoes, sweet potatoes, brown rice, pasta (eat all in moderation)
low-calorie/low-fat butter, olive oil, canola oil, marinara sauce

Snacks

Raw vegetables (with small amount of salad dressing):
carrot sticks
celery sticks
cucumber slices
pickles (low sodium)
air-popped popcorn

Fruit:
fresh or dried cranberries, apricots, raisins, and pineapple
small serving of nuts (8 to 10)
peanut butter and apple slices
sunflower seeds
pistachios
almonds
peanuts

cashews
walnuts
cheese
cheese and crackers
hummus, wheat, or veggie crackers
rice cakes: caramel, cheese, or plain
100-calorie pre-measured snacks
homemade popsicles made from your favorite juices and
fruits
frozen yogurt with fruit toppings

Choose healthy snacks that help you feel full, give you energy, and
stimulate your metabolism.

Desserts

fruits
Jell-O
sherbet
ice cream (½ cup)

Avoid . . .

- Sodas – high in sodium, which causes bloating
- Fried foods – harmful to complexion, can increase body fat
- Unhealthy fast foods and "super-sizing"
- Salt and sugar
- Foods microwaved in plastic containers, which can release harmful toxins

Nutrition charts are now available online for all restaurants.
Make sure you drink plenty of water—keep a bottle with you at all times throughout the day.

Eating well and regularly is the first step to a healthy you. Exercising regularly is the second! As children, we find all sorts of ways to stay active through playtime, recess, neighborhood games, or organized sports. As we grow older, however, we lose the luxury of designated playtime, and we find more and more excuses not to exercise. But staying fit doesn't have to be a regimented chore. Any movement works, whether it's walking, choosing the stairs over the elevator, going for a jog around the school gym, or just taking the dog for a quick walk. With simple exercise, we can help prevent cancers, diabetes, weight gain, and heart disease. It's one of the most important things we can do for our bodies.

Among the many benefits of exercise are reduced stress, less joint and muscle pain, decreased appetite, stronger bones, more restful sleep, and better prevention of "irregularity" and even common colds.

There are all sorts of fun ways to exercise without going to the gym. Here are a few suggestions:

- Kickboxing
- Karate
- Bike riding
- Hiking
- Trail walking
- Jogging
- Hip-hop dancing
- Roller skating
- Tennis
- Swimming
- Volleyball

- Frisbee
- Power-walking around the mall
- Washing the car
- Spending a day at an amusement park
- Hula hooping
- Jumping on a pogo stick or jump rope

Posh Tip: *Thirty minutes of activity a few times a week is a great start to putting your best face forward in the fitness arena. It will help you look and feel your best, inside and out.*

I love the confidence that makeup gives you.

—Tyra Banks

Makeup

Beauty is being comfortable in your own skin. So makeup should be used to enhance your natural beauty, not cover it up or overpower it. When a Miss Universe contestant was asked, "What would you physically change about yourself, and why?" her reply was, "God made me perfect just the way I am." That pretty much sums up how we all should feel about ourselves—we are all beautifully made. Besides, no amount of makeup will ever change who you are on the inside! So when you apply it on the outside, make sure it's done sparingly and for the right reason—to enhance, not to change or attempt to perfect.

Three views on makeup

Kym's thoughts . . .

> I'll admit it. I am a makeup person. I love everything about it—wearing it, applying it, talking about it, and especially buying it! It is a part of my total package, along with hair, skin care, poise, personality, and wardrobe. These are things that some may call "high-maintenance," but for me, they are just a part of my everyday life. Many women consider the whole makeup process too time-consuming, but for me, if it means getting up a little earlier to achieve that well-put-together look, then I'll get up earlier! I see makeup as a wonderful way to enhance your beauty and to make minor flaws disappear. If you know what you're doing, you can define your personal style by the way you wear your makeup.

Chauncey's thoughts . . .

> Some people are makeup people, and some are not. For me, makeup is no more than mascara and lip gloss during the day. But at night and for special occasions, I love for Kym to make me up, because she knows how to use makeup to enhance my natural features. Makeup doesn't make you beautiful; it only enhances the beauty you already possess.

Elouise's thoughts . . .

> When you become older, your makeup should be lighter than it was during your youth. The old saying "Less is more" applies here. I wear makeup every day, but I use it sparingly, making sure to camouflage any dark circles under my eyes. My eye makeup colors are also a little lighter than they used

to be, and I stay away from very dark lipstick. Don't get me wrong, ladies—just because I am a little older doesn't mean I can't have the same class, brass, and sass that I had when I was younger! I'd sooner run naked through the streets than appear in public looking like I was too disorganized or unconcerned to put on makeup!

The basics

When you are first learning to apply makeup, find a quiet place to sit and practice. Don't be afraid to put it on and wipe it off. Makeup isn't permanent—you can easily wash your mistakes right down the drain. Practice makes perfect. Just remember to have fun!

Tools you will need:

- disposable sponges
- eyebrow brushes
- big, soft brushes for powder
- big brushes for blush
- eye shadow brushes
- lipstick brushes
- tweezers
- tissues
- Q-tips
- pencil sharpener
- eyelash curler
- makeup remover
- mirror
- good lighting

Over time you will buy some products and tools that you really like, and some that you'd like to take back for a refund. Don't be afraid to invest in high-quality brushes and other tools; usually the good ones are more expensive for a reason, and they last longer. If you can use something daily for years to come, the initial investment isn't so daunting and can make all the difference in your routine.

Let's get started!

This is your ten-minute beauty makeover. With only one minute for each step, even the busiest of women can take time for this beauty system:

1. Cleanse your face.
2. Moisturize. Before you even think about applying makeup to your face, you have to protect it.
3. Use eye drops to remove any redness before you begin.
4. Apply concealer on dark circles around the eye area and on any small imperfections like pimples or scars. But remember, the best concealer is plenty of water and rest!
5. Use foundation to create the perfect, even canvas for your makeup. Apply lightly for a natural look—it's easier to add a little more than to remove any excess. When applying foundation, blend it downward from the base of your chin toward your neck; no one should see where your foundation starts and ends. Also, make sure the color matches your skin tone. It may be necessary to use two types of lighting when applying foundation. Incandescent light will approximate indoor lighting, while fluorescent lighting is harsher, much like natural sunlight. Use the proper lighting to apply foundation, depending on whether you plan to be indoors or outdoors.

6. Face powder is next. Using a color to match or complement your foundation, powder your face lightly with a large powder puff or brush. Hint: a yellow-based powder matches almost all skin tones beautifully.

7. Groom your eyebrows, if necessary. Eyebrow arching can be one of the most important components of your look, because your eyebrows frame your face and open your eyes. They also can give you a very glamorous look when properly shaped and maintained. The first time you arch your eyebrows, make sure to have them professionally done. There are several different methods professionals use like waxing, tweezing, threading, shaving, depilatories, and a permanent solution, laser treatment. After your brows are professionally arched, you can maintain the shape from then on.

8. Applying eye makeup is the next step. Eye shadows and eyeliner create depth and definition. The lighter the shadow, the larger the eye area looks; the darker the shadow, the smaller the eye area looks. Just lining the top lid opens the eyes; lining the bottom makes them look more almond-shaped. I recommend lining both, which makes them more intense. Mascara can be worn with full eye makeup or by itself to elongate the eyelashes and intensify the eyes. Be sure to reach the inner and outermost lashes of the eye to bring out your entire eye.

9. Apply a bit of blush, which defines your cheekbones and makes you look sun-kissed.

10. Lipstick, lip liner, and lip gloss are the final step. Lip liner defines the lips to look larger or smaller and creates a barrier for your lipstick. The lipstick accentuates and moisturizes your lips while adding a final hint of color to the overall look of your makeup. Gloss adds shine.

Now you have completed your ten-minute makeover. Wasn't that awesome? Beauty enhancement can be quick, and easy, too!

***Posh Tips:** For thicker, fuller lashes, add just a few individual synthetic eyelashes to the corners of your eyes. Strive to keep them natural-looking, and apply mascara as you normally would to your regular lashes. Make sure you use eyelash strip glue and not the permanent kind, so the lashes will be easy to remove.*

For beautiful, pouty lips, line them one shade darker than your lipstick. Then, in the middle of your bottom lip, blend in a shade that is two shades lighter than your lipstick color.

After you finish making up your face, brush a little bronzer or blush over your upper chest for an overall sun-kissed appearance.

Make-up expiration

Believe it or not, makeup does have a shelf life. This isn't just a sinister plot by cosmetics manufacturers to sell more products. Many formulas contain natural ingredients that lose their effectiveness over time. As a rule, the following expiration dates apply:

- foundation — 1 year
- concealer — 1 year
- powder — 2 years
- mascara — 3 to 6 months
- lipstick — 1.5 years
- lip liner or eyeliner — 1 year
- eye shadow — 1.5 years
- powder blush — 2 years
- cream blush — 6 months to 1 year
- creams and lotions — 1 year

Q & A

Q: When should I begin to arch my eyebrows?
A: When you reach your teens. Just remember that once you start, it requires regular maintenance to maintain the desired look.

Q: Can I buy drugstore makeup and still get the quality of a department store brand?
A: Sure, but don't just gravitate toward the cheapest items on the shelves. Quality should still be a consideration. There are some great products you can buy from the drugstore, like Great Lash mascara or individual lashes. The packaging may not be as extravagant as the department store brands, but neither will the price!

I've been doing makeup for such a long time. I was always the girl who did everyone's makeup for prom, photo shoots, or just a night on the town. I love making women look and feel their best. When you feel good about the way you look, you get a new spring in your step, and you can conquer the world with confidence! Makeup should not hide your natural beauty but enhance the beautiful features you were born with. When applied correctly, it boosts your self-esteem and makes you feel as if there's nothing you can't accomplish.

For me, makeup is almost like an accessory; it pulls my look together. But keep in mind that while it can do a lot, makeup is no substitute for adequate rest. That old saying "I have to get my beauty sleep" isn't just a cliché—it's true!

Keep your brushes and utensils clean. Wash them gently at least once a month in warm, soapy water; allow them to dry in a glass with the bristles pointing up. This will keep them beautiful and functional for a long time. Also, make sure your brushes are the best you can afford. Buying good brushes is a great investment, and they should last for years with proper care.

When using sponge applicators, buy a bag and just throw them away after a few uses. Sometimes foundation comes with its own sponge; remember to wash it after every couple of uses. If it is kept inside a compact, the sponge may have a tendency to hold moisture, which can harbor bacteria and cause skin irritation and breakouts.

Always start with a clean face. It is much harder to cover yesterday's smudged eye makeup, and it's not very healthy for your skin, either. Makeup can be your best friend or your worst nightmare, so use it with care. When you are first learning, give yourself enough time to make mistakes and start over. Practice really does make perfect!

Here are a few age-appropriate tips for some of the younger ladies:

Girls aged ten to thirteen should be comfortable with light-colored lip gloss, a small amount of blush on occasion, and maybe a little eye shadow. At this age, not only is it inappropriate to wear heavy or brightly colored makeup, but it's also a time when your skin is very sensitive. You should keep it as clean and fresh as possible to avoid acne and blemishes, so be careful what you put on.

If you're thirteen or older, you might want to try a thin line of eyeliner, a little bit of mascara, and maybe a few more shades of eye shadow, foundation, etc. But again, the cleaner you keep your face, the less chance you have of breaking out. And don't try to look much older than your actual age. Your teenage years are some of the most fun, awesome years of your life. Don't be in a hurry to look or act too grown up, too quickly! You'll have the rest of your life to look like an adult.

Posh Tip: *Whatever your age, and whatever makeup you choose to wear, remember to remove it at night and thoroughly cleanse your face at least twice a day to keep your pores from clogging up. A fresh face with a beautiful smile is always a perfect choice!*

*Long tresses down to the floor can be beautiful if you
have them, but learn to love what you have.*

—Anita Baker

Hair and Nails

To keep your hair looking and feeling healthy, become best friends with your hair stylist and visit the salon regularly. Even if you're fortunate enough to have one of those no-care or low-care hairstyles that require little more than a quick towel-dry after your shower, your appearance can still benefit from regular salon visits.

Can you imagine being a hair stylist, working on your feet all day long? Remember that most salon workers depend on our generosity to make a living wage. So the tip here is "Don't forget to tip!" The amount is up to you, but a good rule of thumb is 15 to 20 percent of your total bill, including a similar percentage for your colorist and a little something for the person who shampoos your hair. Sometimes salon owners do not accept tips, but don't hesitate to ask. Your hair, possibly more than any other external feature, expresses your personality and character. In fact, studies show that along with your smile, your hair is among the first things people notice about you. Fortunately, many traditions and taboos of the past have faded away. The good news is that we no longer have an excuse for a bad hair day. Hairpieces, extensions, braids, ponytails, transplants, wigs, and weaves are all available—and acceptable!

Clean hair is always good, but don't overdo it. You can take the natural gloss and shine from your hair if you shampoo too often or with the wrong products.

Those words on the shampoo and conditioner bottles aren't just marketing slogans. If you have dry, hard-to-manage hair, by all means purchase shampoo that is formulated for "Dry Hair." Chemists have invented wonderful ways of counteracting many hair problems, so don't make the mistake of thinking all shampoos are basically alike.

If you lead an active lifestyle, you may take several showers a day after jogging, tennis, golf, or other exercise. Since nobody wants sweaty, smelly hair, you may be tempted to shampoo each time. Don't! Excessive shampooing can damage your hair. Instead, just run warm water through it, using a small amount of conditioner if necessary. Rinse well, and comb through. This will remove the surface dirt and oils without stripping the hair of its beneficial properties.

If your hair is fine and thin, back-comb it slightly to give it a little more volume. But don't get carried away. Nobody wants "big hair."

Don't lose yourself in the latest fad. What may be the hot new style today may look downright silly on you. Fads come and go; you are better off finding a classic style that fits your face and lifestyle. Keep your style age-appropriate, as well.

Love those hot rollers! They allow you to get dressed while your hair is curling. For long hair, look for super-large rollers that create great wave and bounce so you don't end up with spirally, Shirley Temple-type curls.

Here are some amazing hair facts shared by Dr. Jerry Shapiro at the University of British Columbia Hair Research and Treatment Center:

- Hair is the fastest-growing tissue in the body, second only to bone marrow.
- Thirty-five meters of hair fiber is produced every day on the average adult scalp.
- The average scalp has one hundred thousand hairs. Redheads have the least at eighty thousand; brown—and black-haired people have about one hundred thousand; and blondes have the most at one hundred twenty thousand.
- At any one time, 90 percent of scalp hairs are growing and 10 percent are resting.
- It is normal to lose one hundred hairs per day from the scalp.
- You must lose more than 50 percent of your scalp hairs before it is apparent to anyone.
- Many drugs can cause hair loss.
- Thyroid imbalance and iron deficiency are reversible causes for hair loss.
- More than 50 percent of men have male-pattern hair loss by age fifty.
- Some 40 percent of women have female-pattern (hereditary) hair loss by the time they reach menopause.

Nails

When it comes to manicures and pedicures, you can't beat the spa or salon. All things considered, they offer an inexpensive way to treat yourself, and there is a large selection of spas and salons to choose from wherever you go. They also are a great option for mother/daughter days, outings with girlfriends, and birthdays or other special celebrations. Nothing is more relaxing than having your feet and hands manicured by a professional.

But for those self-reliant souls who like to do their nails at home, here is a quick and basic manicure/pedicure lesson:

1. Wash your hands/feet and remove old polish.
2. Shape your nails.
3. Wash your hands/feet again.
4. Rub each nail with cuticle cream to loosen the cuticle.
5. Clean under the edge of the cuticle with a cotton-tipped orange stick.
6. Use cuticle clippers to trim any hangnails and dead skin.
7. Refine the nail shape and wash hands/feet one more time.
8. Apply base coat.
9. Apply two coats of polish.
10. Apply a clear top coat.
11. Clean up any excess polish around the nail.
12. Allow polish to dry for at least fifteen minutes, and you're done!

FYI: French manicures look awesome, but color is great, too!
FYI: It takes five months for your nails to completely grow out after removing artificial nails or tips.

Keep your nails strong and healthy by following these tips:

• Always file your nails in one direction. Filing back and forth will cause them to split and break.
• Wear nylon or rubber gloves to protect your nails when cleaning or doing dishes.

- Nails grow about an eighth of an inch per month—faster during summer. Your middle fingernail grows most quickly, and your thumbnail grows most slowly.
- Kids' nails grow more quickly than adults', and toenails grow more slowly than fingernails.
- Eating nutritious, balanced meals helps your nails grow and stay healthy.

"Foot"note

Take special care of your feet; they will carry you far enough in a lifetime to have traveled around the world three times. One day when I was doing a fashion show, I saw a model being made up with powder and foundation from head to toe—literally! I took a closer look, and her feet really looked beautiful. The makeup had covered all her unattractive corns and dark spots. (Most models have terrible-looking feet from squeezing them into too-small shoes during runway and fashion shows. I once had to wear shoes that were three sizes too small—worse yet, I had to model them as if they were the most comfortable shoes in the world!) So don't hesitate to use a little foundation on your feet to cover blemishes, and a small amount of powder to set it. This also applies to scars, marks, or bruises on your legs, hips, and chest. Nobody is perfect!

Feet give off odor because they have thousands of sweat glands. Applying powder to your feet before you put on socks will keep your feet dry and odor-free! Another trick is to place dryer sheets inside your shoes or a fresh bar of soap in the closet where your shoes are stored.

Q & A

Q: My hands always seem to be dry. How can I soften them?
A: Try mixing a little mineral oil with your favorite lotion or cream. Do this twice a day, morning and evening.

Q: I feel as if I have not had a real pedicure unless a razor is used on my feet. Is there another way to help soften and smooth them?
A: You may need to have more frequent pedicures until you get your dry skin under control. Pumice stones or foot files are also great, along with salt and sugar scrubs. All these methods will help soften your feet so that a razor will not be needed as frequently.

A note about tipping: The standard gratuity for a manicure/pedicure is 15-20 percent. If multiple technicians serve you, each should receive a separate tip based on the cost of his or her service.

Posh Tip: *Acrylic nails can damage your nail bed and require a lot of maintenance and upkeep. A quick way to add temporary color and design without harming the nail is to purchase inexpensive press-on nails. They may not last as long as artificial nails, but they also won't cause damage and can be changed frequently at minimal cost.*

Like anyone else, there are days I feel beautiful and
days
I don't; and when I don't, I do something about it.

—Cheryl Tiegs

Spa and Salon Etiquette

First of all, nobody—and no "body"—is perfect. We all have
flaws, but a trip to the spa is not the time to concentrate on them. We
defeat the purpose of going to the spa if we can't relax because we're
too busy worrying about what the technician is thinking about our
bodies! Take my word for it—they aren't the least bit interested in
your flaws, because they have flaws of their own, as well. As a trained
cosmetologist aesthetician, I can assure you that the professionals
who serve you at the spa have only one goal in mind: to make sure
you are comfortable and that you receive the best service possible.
If you feel anxious, take a friend with you on your first visit to the
spa. Make it a girls' day out, or use it as an occasion to host a baby
or bridal shower, a special luncheon, or a birthday surprise.

Speaking of birthdays, my husband planned the sweetest birthday bash for me at a local spa. My friends and I arrived not knowing what was in store for us. We were treated to facials and massages and were then led in our plush white bathrobes onto the outdoor terrace, where ten dozen beautiful, long-stemmed roses awaited. Champagne and white chocolate-dipped strawberries were the first course of a light and delicious luncheon. It was the surprise of a lifetime, and one I'll never forget!

Taking the time to go to a spa is mentally and physically therapeutic, but only if you let your guard down and relax.

A few things to remember:

- Be on time or, better yet, early. There is nothing worse than not having enough down time before your treatment begins. Furthermore, your technician is on a schedule, and you may miss part of your session if you are late.
- Turn the cell phone off—not to silent or vibrate, but *off*. Anyone who really needs you will call back or leave a message. Silence is the rule of the day!
- Bring a bathing suit if you are uncomfortable being nude during a steam or Jacuzzi.
- Be sure to give your technician any special instructions, such as not touching your scalp or hair (a possible concern if you wear extensions). Don't be afraid to express yourself if the pressure of the massage is too soft or too deep.
- At the end of your massage, your therapist will quietly leave, suggesting that you enjoy a final few moments of relaxation. Don't lie there too long, as others may be waiting and would like their allotted time, as well.
- Drink plenty of water after your massage to help reduce soreness and replenish any fluids lost during the session.

- Don't forget to tip! If you'd like, you may leave your gratuity at the front desk in a sealed envelope, since the therapist typically leaves the room before you do.
- *Hair stylist: 15-20 percent*

Posh Tip: *You're never too young to learn stress-relieving techniques. Deep breaths, slow counting, exercise, and warm baths all help relieve daily stress. Learn to create your own spa environment at home, where you can relax after a long day at school or play.*

Act as though, and it shall be. The seed you sow today will not produce crop till tomorrow. For this reason, your identity does not lie in your current results. This is not who you are. Your current results are who you were.

—James A. Ray

Finding Serenity at Home

Where at home do you spend the most time? Some would say the kitchen or the bedroom. For a diva, it's the bathroom! Your bathroom should be your haven, your own home spa. It should be a place where you relax, unwind, and become "beautified."

Let's start with ambiance. Keep your sanctuary organized. Invest in storage organizers for your makeup, sponges, towels, soaps, and other pampering essentials. There is no way you can truly unwind if your bathroom is a mess. Keep the lighting as bright as possible for applying makeup and as dim as possible for bathing. Your spa area should reflect you: clean, fresh, and fragrant. Think "soft" when you decorate your bathroom. Soft rugs, soft music, soft towels, and soft lighting from strategically placed candles are all essential for turning your bathroom into your sanctuary.

Enjoying a nice, hot bath allows you to de-stress and reconnect with your inner self. It's amazing how a simple bath can ease your mind, body, and soul. Submerging yourself in hot, bubbly water is therapeutic, unlike a quick shower, which doesn't allow you the time to slow down and enjoy the moment. In the tub you can curl up with your favorite book, listen to your favorite music, or just sit back, close your eyes, and enjoy your favorite aromatherapy candle. You can truly unwind. So indulge and take the time to pamper not just your body but also your soul.

Tea parties

My friends and I *love* tea parties. It's a time when "the girls" can get together and truly be girls, in every sense of the word. Here are some other themed parties that could spark some fun

- Makeup madness party — Invite a makeup artist to demonstrate new cosmetic trends. Allow enough time to try the products, ask questions, and just have fun. Music and chilled beverages add to the festive atmosphere.
- Hat fashion soirée — Give a prize to the girl with the cutest hat.
- Poetry party — Have your guests write a poem, and invite a professional poet to join in, as well. This is a good way to learn the craft from an expert. A good friend of mine did this, and it turned out to be a blast!
- Bring-a-friend party — This is a good way to meet other interesting girlfriends.

- Glam party — Snacks! Manicures! Pedicures! Facials! What a great way to spend time with your girlfriends.

Posh Tip: *Spend some time alone. Take time each day to reflect on your goals, your dreams, and your accomplishments.*

People should start dressing for success before they're successful, not after.

—*Will Smith*

Fashion and Wardrobe

You are what you wear, and that can be awesome—as long as you choose the correct outfit for the right time and the right place. Your choices are a direct indication of how savvy you are. Wear clothes that complement your age, figure, and lifestyle. Keep a fresh, stylish approach to create your individual look.

What do you think is the single most important aspect of your clothing? The color? The cost? A designer label? No! The most important thing to remember when buying and wearing clothes is that the outfit you choose is a reflection of you and the image you want to project.

Girlfriends, do not be intimidated by your wardrobe—or lack thereof. Have some fun learning about fabrics, colors, trends, and workmanship. Simplicity is style, and style is the key to assembling a wardrobe that is funky, fresh, and sassy, yet sophisticatcd.

Wardrobe fundamentals:

1. Take care of your clothing. Keep your clothes clean and pressed.
2. Shoes make a statement all by themselves. Don't scrimp on fashion or comfort. Take care of your shoes by seeing that they are dry and clean before you pack them away. Check them regularly for wear, and find a shoe repair shop you can trust to keep them maintained.
3. Have a little black dress and a basic black suit ready to go at all times. There are no color substitutes for the timeless look of black. From weddings to funerals and everywhere in-between, black will take you there and back. It can be feminine, masculine, or conservative; it's the classic look for all occasions.
4. Accessorize! Try wearing an all-black outfit and adding a splash of color with turquoise or other colorful jewelry for a jazzier vibe, or pearls for a more sophisticated look. You can even pull out the rhinestones for an after-five feel.
5. Investing in quality handbags and shoes will carry you a long way. As long as your handbag and shoes are compatible, you can pair them with almost anything.
6. Quality trumps quantity. I'd rather have one high-quality outfit than five poorly made, less expensive ones.
7. For fuller-figured girls and women, try wearing V-necks, which elongate your body and make you look and feel thinner, rather than round necklines, which can make you look heavier.
8. Finally, the easiest and least expensive item to wear is a smile. Not only will it brighten someone's day, but as our mothers taught us (and Little Orphan Annie reminded us) you're never fully dressed without it!

A final rule of etiquette involves how to get into and out of a vehicle, especially when you're wearing a skirt or dress. Open the door on the sidewalk side, if possible. Swing both legs onto the sidewalk, making sure your legs and feet stay together. Use the side of the door to push yourself up and out of the vehicle. Reverse the process when getting into a vehicle. Sit first, and then swing your legs (together) into the vehicle and turn your body forward. It takes some practice to become "posh" at this technique; however, practice makes perfect!

Q & A

Q: The shoes in my closet are a mess. How can I get them under control?
A: Pull out every pair of shoes you own and get rid of the ones you have not worn in years. (Come on, let go!) Next, buy some plastic shoeboxes, take a photo of each shoe, and tape it to one of the boxes. Now your shoes are ready to be stacked neatly in your closet. (This also keeps your closet smelling fresh!)

Q: I am a size 14. Do I need to wear my clothes bigger so I'll look smaller?
A: No. In fact you should wear garments that fit and show your curves. You do not want to look like a box. The more clothes and layers, the larger you look. The size 2s among us can get by wearing almost anything, but the rest of us need to make sure our clothes fit perfectly.

Q: I love beautiful clothes, but they are so expensive! Where can I shop for quality items without breaking my budget?
A: I like to catch the really great end-of-year sales at some of the retail stores, especially for handbags and accessories. That's when you get the very most for your dollar. For the best selection, go as

soon as the sale starts. And it doesn't hurt to develop a friendship with a knowledgeable sales associate who can give you a call when a big sale is coming up. In the couture departments of the bigger department stores, sales associates still receive commissions or bonuses based on their sales, and they treat their customers well to keep them coming back!

Dress code etiquette

It is so important to be dressed properly, especially for formal events. Think how embarrassing it would be if you showed up at a gala in a casual suit while everyone else was wearing long, elegant gowns.

My advice is, when you get an invitation to a special affair, don't ignore the dress code! The attire should be stated on the invitation, so note that information on your calendar along with all the other details.

What it means . . .

- *Sportswear: swimwear, jogging suits, tennis attire, sandals, shorts, T-shirts, baseball caps — worn to outdoor events or for traveling*

- *Casual: slacks, blouses, sweaters, jeans, leggings — worn to movies, dinner, school, shopping, concerts, some church services/events*

- *Semi-Formal: elegant dresses, jumpsuits, any dress with a length above the ankle (glimmery is appropriate) — worn to evening events, weddings, award ceremonies*

- *Formal/Black Tie: long dresses and evening gowns, glimmer/ glittery attire — worn to proms and cotillion balls, evening weddings, black-tie dinners*

- *White Tie: full-length dress in a rich color and fabric, long gloves — this is the Big One, a state dinner at the White House or dining with royalty*

We must look for ways to be an active force in our own lives. We must take charge of our destinies, design a life of substance, and truly begin to live our dreams.

—Les Brown

Everyday Etiquette

The invitation

The most common cry of hostesses everywhere is, Why don't people RSVP anymore? I honestly wish I knew. There are few things ruder than ignoring an invitation's request to RSVP (*répondez, s'il vous plaît*, or "please reply"). When you receive an invitation, reply as soon as possible. Either call the RSVP number listed on the invitation, or return the RSVP card, if one is enclosed with the invitation. If the invitation states "Regrets only," there is no need to respond unless you cannot attend the event.

Before you leave home

A guest should always be properly attired. If in doubt about what to wear, call the host or hostess ahead of time and ask. (Avoid calling on the day of the affair, as he or she will undoubtedly be quite busy.) When you're invited to a party, it's polite to bring a token gift for the hosts. A thank-you card or flowers are always great choices.

Before you ring the bell

You should be enthusiastic and prepared to treat others as you would like to be treated. It doesn't matter if you had a difficult day; now is the time to put your own concerns aside and think of others. As a guest, you have a responsibility to help make it a lovely event.

If the invitation says 7:00 p.m., you should try to arrive no later than 7:15 or 7:30. Plan ahead for unexpected problems like bad traffic or weather. If you arrive before 7:00, take a leisurely drive through the neighborhood, or park on an adjacent street for a few minutes. Please do not arrive early, since the host or hostess likely needs every bit of time for last-minute preparations. If you arrive late, you should start eating the course of the meal currently being served.

When it is time to leave

Say goodbye to the host and hostess and thank them for a wonderful time. You should have already said a quiet goodbye to your close friends—you don't want to break up the party by making an elaborate exit. Equally important, don't overstay your welcome. It's always best to leave when people don't want you to leave—as opposed to waiting until they do!

Dining out

If you are meeting guests at a restaurant or club and you are the first to arrive, it is customary to wait for them in the lounge or bar area and then request to be seated when your entire party is present. (This eliminates several distracting trips to the table as guests are seated one by one.) In some parts of the country, however, it is customary for unaccompanied ladies to wait at the table, since it is not considered appropriate for them to sit in the bar. Some restaurants, too, would prefer that you wait at the table so the maître d' doesn't have to keep "guarding" it.

Try to determine the most appropriate action for the restaurant you are in. It may be as easy as asking the hostess, "Would you prefer that I wait for my guests at the table?"

On the way to the table

If you spot someone you know, it is okay to wave discreetly or smile and nod. Do not take a detour across the room. If you must have a conversation with your friends across the room, stop by briefly on your way out, or allow them to extend the same gesture if they leave first. If someone you know stops by your table to say hello, do so quickly to keep the aisles clear.

Arriving at the table

Once you arrive at the table, if others are already seated, move around the table to greet each person individually, introducing yourself if you have not met previously. Ladies are typically offered the better seats at the table.

Respect the appearance of the table. Purses, keys, hats, or any other personal item should be left in the car, in your pockets, or with the coat check, or placed on the floor beneath your chair.

Table conversation

In previous eras, the host or hostess would periodically signal "turning the table," which simply meant that if you had been speaking with the person on your right, you would now turn and speak with the person on your left (and vice-versa). That way, everyone was included and nobody was left out. Today, our dinner parties are less structured, but you still should not monopolize the conversation with a single guest. You don't want anyone to feel ignored. Someone once described a seated dinner party as a well-choreographed ballet, in which each "dancer" moves around the table with her eyes and attentions.

Napkins

When you are seated, remove your napkin from the table, unfold it, and place it in your lap. If there is a host or hostess at the table, follow his or her lead. Sit after the hostess sits, place your napkin after she places hers, and so forth. If you leave the table during the meal but plan to return, simply place your napkin neatly on the table, to the left of your plate. The last word on the subject of napkins: never place your napkin on your plate, whether it is linen or paper. Simply refold it casually—don't make it look as if you forgot to use it—and place it to the left of your plate as you prepare to leave the table.

Eating

You will know to start eating when you see the host or hostess do so. (If you are the hostess, please don't make people wait while a guest finishes a long story.) If the food is hot but not all guests have been served simultaneously, the hostess should indicate that those who have been served may start eating. If the course in question is a cold dish like salad or dessert, however, this shouldn't be necessary; everyone should wait to eat until all guests have been served.

As you eat, sit up straight and keep your elbows off the table. Don't hold your knife and fork like daggers, and after you use an eating utensil, it shouldn't go on the table again but should instead rest upon your plate when not in use. Out of consideration for others, avoid making a mess on your plate.

When you are cutting meat, keep your elbows to your side. And don't cut up your entire dinner at one time. (It may seem more efficient, but it looks like you're preparing your plate for a four-year-old.) Put a small amount of food on your fork and take one bite at a time. When you're eating bread, gently pull a bite-sized piece from the dinner roll or baguette and butter it. Don't butter the entire roll or piece of bread at once. And remember: chew with your mouth closed.

When eating soup, use the largest spoon. Ladle the soup away from you, and then gently slide the spoon across the rim of your bowl to remove any excess soup that might otherwise drip from the spoon on its way to your mouth. Eat your soup quietly.

If someone asks you to pass the salt, why make them issue a separate, follow-up request for pepper? The salt and pepper are always passed as a pair, regardless of which was requested. (By the way, don't salt and pepper your food before tasting it. This could be especially offensive in a private home, where the cook is at the table with you.) Keep in mind that in most public settings, food and beverages are served from the left, and plates are removed from the right. And you should always pass to the right.

Take your time

As you eat, try to follow the pace of everyone else at the table. If you are an unusually slow eater, speed it up just a bit out of consideration for the other guests at your table. But remember, you won't get a prize for being the first—or last—to finish!

Problems or complaints

Your waiter is there to serve you and your guests. Don't hesitate to quietly and kindly send something back that is not satisfactory. Don't hesitate to ask for something you want, but try not to be rude when you do. (Remember, it is best not to show "attitude" toward a waiter. He or she is the last person to see your food before it leaves the kitchen. Enough said?)

No matter what happens, it is unforgivably rude to cause a scene in a public place. Shouting, screaming, swearing, or other histrionics will earn you a reputation from which you will never recover. If you have a complaint, you should quietly speak to the maître d' or host (the person who seats you at a restaurant).

Miscellaneous

Don't pick your teeth at the table (or anywhere other than your bathroom, for that matter). If something is caught in your teeth and you can't discreetly dislodge it with your tongue, excuse yourself from the table.

Try not to leave a lipstick trail behind you. Blot your lips before putting a glass to your mouth, but try not to cover your linen napkin with lipstick. Although there are different viewpoints on this, I think it is perfectly acceptable after dinner to quickly and discreetly freshen your lipstick at the table, as long as you don't use a mirror to do it.

If someone is taking medication at the table, no questions are necessary. Also, it isn't necessary to announce that you are going to the ladies' room; just leave quietly.

When you are finished

When you finish eating, your utensils should rest neatly across the center of your plate. Sit quietly until everyone else is finished. Avoid stacking plates to "help" the waiter. Professional waiters are proud of their skills, and they don't need—or want— our help. Placing your hands in your lap makes their job easier when it is time to clear the table.

Tipping

Depending on where you are and the level of service you have received, you should add 15 to 20 percent to the bill, excluding tax. In a situation where you have received extraordinary service, or where you hope for VIP service the next time you return, 25 percent is not unheard of. To compute the tip, look at the subtotal and round up to the next dollar ($132.67 would be $133). Double the first two numbers (13) to get 20 percent (26), or a tip of $26. If you live in a city like

Houston that adds 8.5 percent sales tax to your bill, you can just double the tax on the bill, which gives you a tip amount of almost 17 percent. If I have gotten especially good service, I usually round up from there, so for a meal of $132.67, I would leave an even $30.

An appropriate tip is generally 15 to 20 percent of the bill, excluding tax. Here are tipping guidelines for various professional services:

- Food delivery: 10-15 percent
- Hair stylist: 15-20 percent
- Waiter/waitress: 15-20 percent. If dining at a buffet where you serve your own plate but someone else brings/refills your beverages or condiments, a 10 percent tip is appropriate.

Thank-you notes

Personal thank-you notes should be sent out within a couple of days, and wedding thank-yous should be sent within a few months, not years! When you are invited to a dinner, a thank-you note is definitely appropriate. (Remember to get the personal address beforehand.) E-mailing a thank-you is acceptable, but a handwritten note that comes from the heart adds a more personal touch. It's a great feeling to get a beautiful, handwritten note of appreciation—it makes you feel special. Write your thank-you note as if you're talking to the person. And be neat; use a straightedge or ruler, if necessary, to avoid crooked, illegible writing.

Utensils for the properly set table

Dinner plate
Charger plate (optional)
Salad plate or bowl
Bread plate

Water glass
Beverage glass
Tea or coffee cup and saucer
Salad fork
Dinner fork
Knife
Butter knife
Soup spoon
Dessert or teaspoon
Placemat
Napkins

Remember: with silverware, you should start from the outside of the place setting and work your way in.

Lunch Etiquette

If you say, "Let's do lunch," then follow up and do lunch. Don't be the one to drop the ball with unkept promises. Do not be late, *please!* You don't want the other person to feel that your time is more valuable than his or hers. And do not be a gossip. There is so much more to talk about than someone else's business.

Q & A

Q. When you are an overnight guest at someone's home, what do you do with the soiled bedding?
A. Before you leave, it is appropriate to remove the sheets and pull the comforter up. Soiled bedding should be folded neatly and placed at the end of the bed or taken to the laundry room.

Q. When invited to dinner or a party, can I bring a friend?
A. Not unless the invitation includes "guest" or you've received permission from the host beforehand. There may be limited budgets or seating involved.

Q. I hate to leave my small pet at home alone. Is it okay to bring it with me to a party or dinner?
A. Absolutely not.

Q. May I return a housewarming gift?
A. It's okay to return the gift if it really does not suit your style. However, to avoid hurting any feelings, you need not let anyone

know. Remember, though, if this guest visits your home again, he or she may wonder what happened to the gift. Use discretion and careful consideration.

Trying to find just the right gift? Try birthstone colors

January garnet
February amethyst
March aquamarine
April diamond
May emerald
June pearl or alexandrite
July ruby
August peridot
September sapphire
October tourmaline or opal
November topaz or citrine
December tanzanite, zircon, or turquoise

A final rule of etiquette involves how to get into and out of a vehicle, especially when you're wearing a skirt or dress. Open the door on the sidewalk side, if possible. Swing both legs onto the sidewalk, making sure your legs and feet stay together. Use the side of the door to push yourself up and out of the vehicle. Reverse the process when getting into a vehicle. Sit first, and then swing your legs (together) into the vehicle and turn your body forward. It takes some practice to become "posh" at this technique; however, practice makes perfect!

Posh Tip: *An appropriate tip is generally 15 to 20 percent of the bill, excluding tax. Here are tipping guidelines for various professional services:*

- *Food delivery: 10-15 percent*
- *Waiter/waitress: 15-20 percent. If dining at a buffet where you serve your own plate but someone else brings/refills your beverages or condiments, a 10 percent tip is appropriate.*

Remember that your phone does have an off button.
There are very, very few things in the world that
absolutely cannot wait.

—Anonymous

Electronic Etiquette

Cell phone etiquette

Cell phones are one of the greatest inventions, providing convenience, ready help in emergencies, and an easy way to keep in touch during our busy lives. However, there is a time and place for everything, including our phones.

If you're at a restaurant, movie, meeting, school, or office building, your phone should be turned to silent or vibrate. I would even suggest turning it off *completely* during church, but I realize that many people now prefer using Bible apps on their phones in order to search scriptures during service rather than carrying heavier, bulkier Bibles. Nevertheless, use discretion to avoid causing distractions during a service. Ringtones should be turned off, and under no circumstances should you read or respond to a text message—you are still in church!

When you're out and about on your cell phone, no one wants to hear you cursing, nor are they interested in your personal business. Keep your voice low any time you are in a public setting or where others may overhear your conversation, and be considerate enough not to use the speakerphone option when others are around, unless you are suggesting a group conversation.

If you are with others, do not keep them waiting while you finish a lengthy phone conversation; tell the caller you'll call him back shortly. If it's imperative that you take a call, excuse yourself from the table or group and complete your conversation out of earshot of the other guests. Try to end it as quickly as possible in order to get back to the group or person.

Also, answering a call or text while talking to someone is the same as turning your back or walking away from her while she is in mid-sentence. It's rude and unacceptable. If you are expecting an important call, let the person you are with know in advance so she'll understand when the call does come.

Rules of cell phone etiquette would seem to be common sense, but it's surprising how people act (and react) sometimes.

Realize that calls on a cell phone can drop off if either party is driving, walking, or moving about—especially inside buildings. Some structures are designed to block phone signals, which can interfere with equipment used inside the building. If a call drops, the person who initiated the call should call back. If you know it was your phone that disconnected, call or text the other party to explain and apologize, and offer to call back later when you can get a signal. Never blame someone for a call that drops, because he or she may not be able to control the situation.

If someone else (like your parent or employer) is paying for your phone and/or service, courtesy dictates that you should answer your phone whenever he calls you, even if it means putting someone else on hold. After all, he is the one paying the bill. And if you're lucky enough to own a smart phone that allows Internet access and multitasking, avoid browsing, texting, and Googling while on a call with someone. Your focus should be on the call.

Cell phones should not be used to record conversations unless the other person is aware you are doing so and has agreed to be recorded.

A word about ring tones: there are some really fun, interesting ones available, so you can pick and choose from a variety and change them as often as you'd like. The rule to remember here is to pick something appropriate and un-annoying, especially if you're one of those people who tends to leave your volume turned up and then walk away from your phone. Nothing is more bothersome at work, school, or elsewhere than to hear someone else's aggravating ring tone playing over and over because she stepped into another room and didn't think to turn down the volume on her phone before leaving. If you work or study in an open environment or cubicle setting, your phone should remain on vibrate or silent as a courtesy to those around you.

The World Wide Web

If you're computer savvy—and probably even if you're not—you're familiar with the World Wide Web. After all, everything is "www-this" and "www-that." Remember, though, that it's called "World Wide" for a reason: because it reaches around the world! That's good and bad. Everything—and I do mean everything—that you do online is out there . . . somewhere. Every keystroke that is transmitted via Internet is traceable to some degree. Once you hit "send" and it's out there, you can't take it back. Somehow, some way, somewhere, someone can retrieve it. So if you don't want your parents, spouse, pastor, boss, or anyone else to see something, then it's probably not appropriate to post. As big as our world is, you'd be surprised how quickly news will beat you home! Someone you know always knows someone else you know—someone whom you may not want to know your business. If that's the case, keep it to yourself, or save it for a private conversation—offline and out of earshot and eyesight of the World Wide Web.

Schools, employers, and law enforcement all use the web to search for information. No matter how secure and private you think your social network pages are, be assured someone you least expect has access to them, or has access to a "friend" who has access to them. Posting about skipping school or cheating on tests, or bad-mouthing friends/teachers/co-workers online is *never* a good idea. More than one court case has been won, or lost, because information posted on social media is admissible as legal evidence. Beware . . . be warned . . . be careful . . . and be smart about what you post!

Whether you're calling, texting, posting, or e-mailing, here are some simple rules to remember:

- o Electronic media should be an alternate form of communication, not a replacement for face-to-face interaction. "Face time" with friends, family, and others is an important part of a healthy relationship and social environment.
- o Always make sure you're texting/calling/e-mailing the right person. It's really embarrassing to send a message to someone you never intended to receive it!
- o Respond to texts/voice mails/e-mails as quickly as possible—at least within twenty-four hours. If you don't want to be bothered by the person, then politely ask him to stop calling/texting/e-mailing you.
- o Sharing private texts/voice mails/e-mails with others is similar to gossiping. Be mindful of what you share with others and whether or not the information was meant to be shared.

o Realize that anything you text/e-mail/post could end up in the wrong hands. If you don't want anyone to see that risqué photo of you in your lingerie, then don't send or post it. You'd be surprised where some pictures end up!

o If you receive a message not intended for you, politely respond and let the sender know that you believe you received it in error. This allows him to correct his mistake and send it to the proper person.

o If you text or e-mail someone who is unfamiliar with your cell phone number or e-mail address, clearly identify yourself early in the message. Different phones transmit text messages in different ways. If you have a lot to say, understand that your message may be truncated or split on the other end. Give people time to read and respond to your first text before sending out another. It's aggravating if you're trying to read or respond to a text while new messages are coming in.

o Abbreviations are fine, but make sure they are understandable. And while texts don't have to be perfectly written, avoid too many mistakes, curse words, etc., that can make them difficult or unpleasant to read.

o Know that texting/e-mailing/posting should never replace face time with friends or be used for important topics. E-mails pertaining to work or school should be grammatically correct, as they are a reflection of your professionalism. You should always put your best foot forward in any communication.

o Always take time to review and proofread your texts and e-mails before you hit "send." If you question whether the content reflects your feelings or may be too harsh or to the point, I suggest you sit on it for a few hours and then come back, reread, and make your decision whether or not to send.

o Avoid sending e-mails that threaten bad luck if the recipient doesn't forward the e-mail to a specific number of people. Most people are offended by such suggestions.

o   Be considerate of others' schedules. Don't assume that because you are awake, working, or not busy, the person you're texting is, as well. Nobody wants her sleep interrupted by recurring beeps or buzzes. Of course, the flip side of that is to silence or turn off your phone whenever you don't want to be bothered. You have that control!

Here are some common abbreviations used in texting:

- LOL – laugh out loud
- OMG – oh my gosh / oh my goodness
- ROFL – rolling on the floor laughing
- SMH – shaking my head
- TTYL – talk to you later
- IJS – I'm just saying . . .
- BFF – best friend forever
- ADR – address
- AEAP – as early as possible
- ALAP – as late as possible
- ASL – age/sex/location
- CD9 – Code 9 (parents are around)
- C-P – sleepy
- F2F – face-to-face
- HAK – hugs and kisses
- ILU – I love you
- MOS – mom over shoulder
- NMU – not much, you?
- P911 – parent alert
- PAL – parents are listening
- PAW – parents are watching
- PIR – parent in room

Posh Tip: *Cyber-bullying is unacceptable and should be taken very seriously. If you're threatened online, never try to get even with the bully; instead, contact an adult to review the threats and take the appropriate action.*

Choice, not chance, determines your destiny.

Jean Nidetch

Ageless Beauty

A respectful attitude goes a long way in allowing beauty to shine through you. Being confident around others, and taking the initiative to introduce yourself and those around you, shows not only maturity and kindness but a strong, confident you.

When you are introducing two people with a noticeable difference in their ages or positions, always begin by addressing the older or more senior person—for example, "Aunt Sally, this is my classmate, Victoria. Victoria, this is my Aunt Sally." If you forget a name during the introduction, don't make a big deal about it, which will just cause embarrassment. Simply say something like, "Aunt Sally, this is my classmate." Chances are your classmate will then extend her hand and say, "Hello, my name is Victoria," or perhaps Aunt Sally will say, "Hi, nice to meet you. I didn't catch your name." Another rule of thumb is to address a lady or girl before a man or boy.

Here are some titles to help you remember a person's position as you address or introduce him or her:

o *Mr.* is a man, usually over the age of sixteen.
o *Master* is a boy or young man under the age of sixteen.
o *Mrs.* is a married woman, regardless of age.
o *Miss* in an unmarried woman, often reserved for women under the age of forty.
o *Ms.* refers to a woman, married or unmarried. The term may be used by young women who don't want to be identified or classified by marital status, or by older women who are single and feel that *Miss* is a bit too juvenile.
o When introducing a married couple with the same last name, refer to them as *Mr. and Mrs.* If they are married but do not share the same last name, introduce them as *Mr. So and So and his wife, Ms. Such and Such.*

Ageless beauty is about more than just your outer appearance. It is about your confidence and the faith you have in yourself to be you. Enjoy this season of your life. Live well.

Uplifting your girlfriends

Girlfriends, there is no reason to be jealous of one another. If someone else has something you want, buy it, or save up until you can! If someone has long hair and you want it, you can buy it—really! Also, make sure that what you want is really *for you*; we have to learn to appreciate what we have and understand that not everything is for us to have. But don't resent someone else for having it. Instead, work hard and be persistent; there is nothing you cannot achieve in this life if you have the right attitude.

It's time we girls look out for each other and uplift one another. We need to establish new, wonderful bonds with one another and create the reputation that women are kind, thoughtful, and supportive of their girlfriends. If someone "has it going on," compliment her rather than talking behind her back, which will only make you feel worse in the long run, anyway. If you "have it going on," share your secrets of success with your girlfriends; don't try to keep all the glory for yourself. And if you don't have anything nice to say about someone, as the saying goes, "don't say anything at all."

Your friendships with other women should be a blessing and one of the best parts of your life. Learn to embrace each other, physically and emotionally.

Posh Tip: *Don't let a little dispute injure a great friendship. When you realize you've made a mistake, take immediate steps to correct it. And never laugh at anyone's dreams. People who don't have dreams don't have much.*

Tend to your roots

Have you ever taken the time to think about the roots of a tree—what they do and how they work? The roots of any plant provide critical life support to keep it healthy and strong. They enable a tree to stay grounded through storms and wind and supply it with the nutrients and water from the soil that are needed for survival. Sometimes plants must produce new roots, exploring new areas of soil, in order to acquire more nutrients and grow larger and stronger. Trees must also produce roots to replace old roots that have died, were lost to predation, or no longer function well.

Why is this important? Like the tree, you also have roots—your mind, heart, and soul. These are the life-support system that help sustain you through triumph and tragedy. They give you what you need to maintain a healthy "you," physically, spiritually, and emotionally. It is your duty to tend to your roots!

Like a plant, you may need to grow new roots in order to expand and explore. Whether this is feeding your mind through reading, or strengthening your soul through prayer, friendship, and laughter, it is your job as gardener to make sure the root in you stays nurtured and healthy. So do things that make you feel good—wake up early and just go! You don't need a destination; spontaneity fuels the inner spirit and allows you to feel free. Even if you're sitting at home with nothing to do, get dressed and look your best. Looking good makes you feel good, and you have to learn to smile from the inside out.

Never let your roots get weak. Keep your inner self full; never let it get past, or even close to, empty. We women naturally tend to the growth and well-being of others and forget to replenish our own selves. So remember to fill your mind with knowledge, your heart with love, and your soul with laughter. You are the gardener, and you possess the tools to keep your roots healthy and your garden growing!

Thoughts from Mom ...

I have always tried to take care of myself so that I would look and feel young for as long as possible, and I think it has worked! When I turned sixty, I started noticing some signs of age and seeing things that required prioritizing in my beauty regimen. We owe it to ourselves to enjoy life. If we take care of ourselves while we are young, we will always enjoy an ageless, fruitful life.

Part of taking care of yourself is recognizing that you are what you eat, and eating properly must become a lifestyle. There's an old adage by Socrates that says, "Eat to live, not live to eat." I have tried to follow this rule, and I encourage you to do the same. Instead of turning to food for pleasure, look and find your joy, whether it is sitting down to read a good book, driving to the beach and smelling the wonderful salt water, or taking a couple of days to go shopping in Los Angeles, New York, Dallas, Chicago, or Florida—shop 'til you drop!

Wise Advice

- o Get plenty of rest.
- o Drink plenty of water.
- o Keep good, clean thoughts.
- o Be appreciative all God has given you.
- o Take care of your health.
- o Get regular checkups.
- o Get eight hours of sleep each night,
- o Exercise as much as possible.
- o Get plenty of fresh air,
- o Walk as often as possible,
- o Have daily quiet time; meditate, if possible, and seek spiritual peace.
- o Give love, and you will receive it in return.

Ageless beauty is about more than just your outer appearance. It is about your confidence, and the faith you have in yourself to be you. Enjoy this season of your life. Live well, and use the wisdom and strength you have acquired to help yourself and others live with ageless beauty!

YOUR CLEANSING THOUGHTS

There is an old saying I was taught as a child. "Pretty is, as pretty does." But the true essence of a beautiful woman comes from the dept of her heart and soul. Look from within yourself to fulfill your potential, but most of all is be true to yourself.

Share your joy, count your blessings and spread your happiness out into the world.

As the true you is unveiled and you embrace your inter light your eyes will be opened and others will see that compassion and love for life you radiate from the inside out.

Upon finding this precious gift of inner beauty and peace we can share with others, through a smile, clean living, wholesome thoughts, a giving spirit of kindness, love and understanding,

I'm convinced that if we truly believe from the bottom of our hearts and soul to live life with Joy, Faith and Compassion, treating people the way we wish to be treated and if we all give each other our best what a wonderful and beautiful world this would be to live in.

Powder Puff Principles Notes

Powder Puff Principles Notes

Powder Puff Principles Notes

The *Powder Puff Principles* Books

One of the fondest memories I have from my childhood is watching my grandmother go through the daily process of her morning beauty routine. I can remember, as if it were yesterday, the powder puff dusting she gave her entire body, leaving behind a glorious scent, and the second dusting of her beautiful, kind, delicate face just made her beauty all the more evident to me.

My grandmother had other beauty secrets, I am sure, but that powder puff ritual stands out in my mind—so much so, that it inspired the name of this book. My grandmother's powder puff represented everything that was refined, gracious, elegant, and endearing to me. She always seemed to be effortlessly manicured and under control in almost any situation. There seemed to be nothing she could not handle. She had a simply classic quality of prevailing grace—and to my youthful sensibilities, it all stemmed from that fluffy, pink powder puff that glided so elegantly across her face and body!

Grandma's beauty regimen reflected her approach to life: clean, fresh, simple, energetic.

Powder Puff Principles is about remembering the grace and good manners our mothers and grandmothers displayed in their dress, behavior, and the image they projected, while preparing ourselves to do the same for our children.

Powder Puff Principles is about being polished and prepared, and adhering to morals and integrity. These principles allow us to embrace our own strengths and femininity while empowering us to do anything we put our minds to!

Acknowledgments

First, I would like to thank our Heavenly Father for his guidance and patience. Thank you also to my beautiful family and friends for the love and support you have given me.

Mom, you have been my constant source of strength and my biggest fan ever since I can remember. I'm truly grateful that God blessed me with you as my mother.

Will, Blake, Mary, and Chauncey—may you never stop reaching for your hopes and dreams. I love you with all my heart and soul!

Cookie and Carol, you mean the world to me! Mirna, Meaghan, JaCarous, Gena, and Tiffany, your friendship is invaluable. A special thank-you for consistent love, guidance, and support to AJ Johnson and Peggy Shawaker. Thank you for your beautiful enlightenment, Dereck, Crystal, Donnell, Kena, Shirelle, Dvyne, Karen, Wanda, Evelyn, and Marcia.

Anne, thank you for your kindness and support. You have helped shape my thoughts and bring them to life!

Willard—my husband, my friend, my love—you are my dream come true! After twenty-six years, it still feels new. Thank you for being open to my dreams. I love you, sweetheart.

Bibliography

- *The Guide to Good Manners for Kids* / Emily Post
- *The Bad Girl's Scrappy Book* / Cameron Tuttle
- *Total Beauty* / Sarah Stacey and Josephine Fairley
- *The Fabulous Girl's Guide to Decorum* / Kim Izzo and Ceri Marsh
- *Giving Birth to Me* / Dawne Kirkwood
- *Unleash the Winner Within You* / Patrick E. Alcorn
- *From the Soul of a Woman* / Valorie N. Parker
- *Live Your Dreams* / Les Brown
- *The Official Book of Electronic Etiquette* / National League of Cotillions

About the Author

Kym Jackson has been passionate about charm and etiquette since she entered the world of pageantry at age seventeen, going on to win "Mrs. Texas" in 2007. She received a bachelor of arts in fashion and fine arts in 1986, and her entrepreneurial spirit and business acumen have led her to own boutiques, day spas, and salons across the country. She has been a makeup artist and stylist for videos, plays, television, and photo shoots for many high-profile personalities.

Kym is also a licensed cosmetologist and medical aesthetician and is now studying for her GIA certification.

This is Kym's fourth book. She also has her own jewelry collection, "Unique Urban Rocks," which can be found at specialty boutiques in the Beverly Hills and Houston areas. Kym volunteers with The Rose Ribbon Foundation, the Autism Speaks Foundation, and The American Heart Association.

Kym enjoys traveling, golf, and arts and crafts. She resides in Houston, and she adores her husband, Willard L. Jackson, three children, Will, Blake, and Chauncey, and one granddaughter, Harley.

Powder Puff Principles
A posh girl's guide to etiquette